Renaming the Streets

POEMS BY
JOHN STONE

Louisiana State University Press
Baton Rouge and London
1985

Designer: Christopher Wilcox
Typeface: Galliard
Typesetter: G&S Typesetters, Inc.

Library of Congress Cataloging in Publication Data

Stone, John, 1936–
  Renaming the streets.

  I. Title.
PS3569.T6413R46   1985   811'.54   85-11289
ISBN 0-8071-1271-2
ISBN 0-8071-1272-0 (pbk.)

Grateful acknowledgment is made to the following publications in which
some of the poems first appeared: *American Scholar, Annals of Internal Medi-
cine, Chattahoochee Review, Medical Heritage, Midwest Quarterly, Patterns of
Poetry, Southern Poetry Review*. "Three for the Mona Lisa" and "You Round
the Bend" first appeared in the August, 1982, issue of *Poetry*. "January: A
Flight of Birds" was initially printed, in slightly different form, as a broad-
side, by Palaemon Press in 1983.

"Gaudeamus Igitur" was previously published in the *Journal of the American
Medical Association*, CCXLIX (April 1, 1983), 1741–42; copyright © 1983,
American Medical Association; reprinted by permission.

Publication of this book has been supported by a grant from the National
Endowment for the Arts in Washington, D.C., a federal agency.

for John Ciardi
for Miller Williams

in honor of Magpie Lane (formerly Grove Street)

Contents

Renaming the Streets

Early Sunday Morning

Somewhere in the next block
someone may be practicing the flute
but not here

where the entrances
to four stores are dark
the awnings rolled in

nothing open for business
Across the second story
ten faceless windows

In the foreground
a barber pole, a fire hydrant
as if there could ever again

be hair to cut
fire to burn
And far off, still low

in the imagined East
the sun that is again
right on time

adding to the Chinese red
of the building
despite which color

I do not believe
the day
is going to be hot

It was I think
on just such a day
it is on just such a morning

that every Edward Hopper
finishes, puts down his brush
as if to say

As important
as what is
happening

is what is not.

Rosemary

Little Rock, Arkansas
October 26, 1982

6 A.M. All over the world
people are sleeping in shifts.
Rosemary is my waitress.

Not only is she beautiful
she brings me food and herbs
from the stores of her pantry.

From the looks of her
the legs are the last to go.
To, fro, she has a most remarkable walk

anatomy-proud, pendulum-perfect.
Does she have children
a husband   asleep

off somewhere in this remote new day?
It's ill-advised to ask such questions
yet they're what I'd like to know

after an evening
in the arms of the Sheraton.
Last names are never put

on name tags now
have you noticed?
They could be used as proof.

Besides
a last name is too intimate.
A name tag like *Rosemary*

is properly civil
opaque as a servant.
I tell her my name is John.

There is a buffet
which I approach under the gaze
of a Jack O'Lantern

set up against those
who would take too much bacon.
I choose freely, with the magical joy

of hunger, taking some extra bacon
and stroll back with my plate.
There is so much

I'd like to have Rosemary tell me
but she pirouettes
constantly, table to table

pouring coffee,
resetting the places
for the other nameless

numb nightcrawlers
descended from
their Posturized beds

into the subdued light
of this morning place.
The businessmen

are reading the grim papers,
wiping their mouths, leaving,
a gnaw now in their upper abdomens.

My fourth cup of coffee
is strong, doing
its intravenous work.

Suddenly I realize that Rosemary and I
are alone in this place.
She sits herself down

at a table across the room
to have her own quick breakfast.
The sun is coming in through her hair.

I want to call her over, say
Rosemary, sit down
then read her this poem.

But there is no such thing
as a simple pleasure.
I have the feeling she knows

it is already too late for poems.
All over Little Rock
in great Brownian motion

all of the others
are waking up
just as we feared they would.

January: A Flight of Birds

Watching the birds, I think of Bach,
each of the distant wheeling flock

a black note on a turning page,
the darkened afternoon the stage.

Watching their wide, then narrow belt
I imagine how Bach felt,

with hundreds of melodies all at once,
inventing his own celestial stunts.

In their equivalent of cantata,
the birds perform a short fermata

then in silent sky-bound bugle
swoop and go, their music fugal.

I think of their flight in terms of Master
Bach at his keyboard, writing vaster

harmonies than the court could dream—
which is why, in pure esteem,

the world would be, if Bach- and bird-less,
as much diminished as if wordless.

The Storm

for Marjorie and for Mel

Someone on the tallest spot in town
first looking up, then gazing down
would have seen
the gods get very angry, as my friend
the anthropologist would say

for clouds that looked as though they meant to stay
rumbled in from the west, a mottled blend
dark-blue and mean
announced by rain and wind if one were blind
and moving the shoppers down below to find

some cover—or open one, as domed and mute
mushroomed umbrellas gave salute
to this machine
the deadly wrath and power of the gods
each wanting his way—or hers—in the world below

and each of us here wanting only to know
what he or she had done; and what were the odds
that this obscene
wild message from afar
was meant for them
already the subjects of one hot star
already drowning in the water we mostly are.

Forecast

I can wade Grief—
Whole Pools of it
—Emily Dickinson

It started raining Grief tonight
in purest barometric blunder—
hard Grief, merciless, despite

the forecast—which made me wonder
why we of all had to be chosen—
but since Grief fell from such a height

and since the darkness now is frozen,
that Grief is turning into snow,
crunching underneath our feet

quieting the traffic's flow
taking the shapes of our charades
until the sun compels its rise

as Grief and Light must always meet
and the temperature persuades
Grief's slow invisible demise.

is more
than the sum
of her parts

her breath
sleep   her walk
her lup

dup
not to mention
of course

her unmentionables
such
as

her brain waves
delta and alpha
which go on

and on
and which
like the smell

of her hair
have been carefully
recorded.

Intrigue at the Office

Oh, he was a happy man,
never a day off did he shirk;
no one ran faster than he ran
to stay out of the way of work.

And *Oh* and *Wow* the game he talked
when new projects were being planned;
when they started, though, he balked:
his part was always undermanned.

Some days he couldn't find anything—
nothing was in its predicted place;
nor could Hercules in full swing
bring any order, much less grace—

his desk in geologic stages
from NOW to THEN to I FORGET.
Despite his quite substantial wages,
his files defied the alphabet.

This morning, though, the place was changed,
the desk and its credenza neat;
the new day's calendar arranged—
in short, a miracle, complete

with shining nameplate on the door
and all the papers in a stack;
and, after a search of a month or more,
the long-lost scissors, lodged in his back.

The Hands

The Emergency Department is usually quiet early Saturday mornings. Things that hurt too badly have caused the owners of such pain to come in earlier—and the accidents haven't as yet had time to happen. But the early morning is a favorite time for the elephant-on-the-chest discomfort of a heart attack: it may come on during the rapid eye movement portion of sleep, that part of sleep associated with dreaming. With a thumping dream, good or bad, the eyes roll under the lids like marbles in oil. It can be as though you're running while lying down, your body tense, heart pumping wildly to no purpose, blood pressure up. Perhaps that's when it happened to him.

What we know is that he sat up on the side of the bed, still, as when he went to sleep, 39 years old. And complained of pain. An ambulance was called and got to him quickly: no question what he had or what must be done. Lying there, hurtling there under the siren, he stopped breathing. Resuscitation was begun: pump, breathe, pump, breathe. Two minutes from the hospital. Radio the Emergency Department: *Roger. Man with chest pain. Just arrested. ETA 1 minute. Get the doors open.*

Galvanized is the word for what happens then in the Emergency Department: a flurry of white coats, hands, legs, linen. Drugs, EKG ready. The whip of the siren. *They're on the ramp.*

39, I keep thinking. *Damn!*

As the EKG machine is hooked up, the tube for breathing pure oxygen is put down. *He's pinker. Keep pumping on the chest.* Nothing on the EKG. Not a thing, just the mechanical jumps of the needle as the Resident pumps a perfect 60 times a minute. Nothing to shock. Flat line. Drugs—that's what we need: *epinephrine, bicarb. Hurry. Keep pumping!*

The Resident is sweating heavily and is relieved when someone offers to take over for him. Nothing works. No drug is helping. Try another. *Try calcium.*

I swear his hand moved—no, his *arm* moved. *Both* arms are moving! His heart still dead, but he's moving his arms! *God. Never Saw That Happen Before.*

The hands come up on his chest to the hands of the pumping Resident and *push* them away. He's making a sound around the tube in his mouth.

Check the EKG. Stop pumping. Check it.

Nothing.

The hands fall down lifeless again. Pump.

Pump! Try some more epinephrine. Nothing. Straight line. Nothing on his own.

Get me a pacemaker.

The hands come up again, pushing away the doctor's hands.

Stop pumping so I can see the EKG. Nothing. The man's hands fall down again as the pumping is interrupted momentarily. We're keeping him alive but he won't let us.

Here's the pacemaker. Keep pumping. Check the blood gases.

The pacemaker doesn't help. He has no pump left. His heart muscle is gone. We keep trying, pumping. The hands come up and fall back down. Death is fighting off life and the living.

We work for hours. The hands are weaker; they do not rise as often; they do not rise at all; they do not move. We have lost in spite of everything. The something that waits inside us all for the first falter and stumble of the heart has won.

I hope his wife is a strong spirit. I'd like to tell her about the hands. About how he struggled. How we hurt with him in that purgatory until we were all rendered innocent of everything we might have been guilty of, then and tomorrow.

of the expressway
just at dusk
there is something in the road

as you hurtle toward it
all you know is
that you want it not to be

something that ever had
the possibility
of loving

because
whatever it is
it's dead

And it's unavoidably
under your wheels
It's a rolled-up carpet just

a carpet, old and worn
You drive on, taking in
and letting out a sigh because

you know that such a circumstance
can be complicated
and you are glad

this once that it isn't.

Trying to Remember Even a Small Dream
Much Less the Big Gaudy Ones in Color
with Popcorn and High Ticket Prices

As soon as you wake up

but before the first photon
has leaped through the black pupil
to the back of your eye

before you sit heavily to the day
at the side of your mattress

be on the lookout:

your last dream may just then
be disappearing
into the kingdom
of your lateral gaze

You may be able to recognize
one of the full-blown characters
if you can catch sight of his shoes
the flare of her dress
the cut and color of her hair

Then there's always the possibility

that your dream itself
may pause a moment
to look back at you

rubbing the sleep from its eyes

wondering how it got inside you
as its mother warned it might

amazed
that it too ended up

so far from home.

The Eclipse

Atlanta
May 30, 1984

The day of the eclipse began like any other.
I'd thought one god or another might call it off.
By eleven, though, the sun high, I guessed

they were planning to go on through with it.
Already, crowds of people with smoked glass,
armed with blankets, chairs, beer and wine

against the universe, were swarming their curious
ways to the open country of the park.
Only a limited amount of work can be done

on a day scheduled to be cut in half,
making two holidays where there were none. I went
along as disbeliever to watch what clearly

was out of my hands. There was nothing brusque
about what happened next. Only the sun
dependably overhead and hot—and then

the slow diminuendo wash of dusk:
a perceptible chill, a slight moon-lit wind,
all the gullible street lamps coming on,

the birds ruffling in uneasy slurs,
tree to tree. Then false dawn, in which
those trees relearned their shadows. And it was over.

A woman was heard to say *It didn't last
long enough*. *It never does*, I said.
But what we all remembered most was the drunk

who'd waited both days and most of his life to ask
those of us still lounging in the park,
as the real sun was relentlessly going down:

Is this the eclipse? Or is it just getting dark?

Seeing Double After Eye Surgery

for Sister Bernetta Quinn

Neither eye nor brain
is fooled by ruses

Such is their love
their work together

that what is false
is false to both

Until they move
in perfect tether

they act upon
a common oath:

In their art
they are the Muses

by which our vision,
should it not fuse,

chooses.

Standing here, endless, alone on the shore
talking to myself, trying to remember
stories I'm afraid I may forget

I am not at all impressed by myth
What's so special for instance
about Sisyphus

and his recalcitrant rock
Which of us doesn't
have his own big stone

to roll repeatedly up his own hill?
The typist returns each morning
to the same illogical set of keys

The bus driver reports again
to the permanently indented seat
of his monster

The pianist rehearses once more
the 88 sounds of
someone else's name

The cardiologist
back at his stethoscope
half-expecting to have to say

would you repeat that please
hears only the heart
restamping the tickets

for the return trip.
And the ships and the planes
I know are out there somewhere

far   flung
their men and women
are as bored as the horizon

If any of this
could be changed   by a letter
a phone call   a message in a bottle

they do not come.
Even the sea
repenting

keeps making the same
very old
excuses

Three for the Mona Lisa

1

It is not what she did
at 10 o'clock
last evening

accounts for the smile

It is
that she plans
to do it again

tonight.

2

Only the mouth
all those years
ever

letting on.

3

It's not the mouth
exactly

it's not the eyes
exactly either

it's not even
exactly a smile

But, whatever,
I second the motion.

The Answer

Where does the time go?
—question posed in a letter

I know this much
none of it is lost.
I have reason to believe
it is changed into
whatever is needed

Some of it is used
to patch up
old worn-out
mantras

It makes up
that part of diastole
the heart does not need
for rest

fills the space
between Good-bye
and Hello

It is the rest
of the dream
you woke from

It is that part
of the light
that goes into the mirror
but never comes
back out

It is inhaled while
enduring
the broken accordion of traffic

spread by word of mouth

missed mostly
at breakfast
while coming to grips
with the fact
that it's Monday

It is what little girls
are made of
It is why little boys
are afraid

It is frittered away
like confetti
on the heroes of our
second, third, and fourth
puberty

stuffed into
the corners of a late
Fall afternoon

glows in the fireplace

It is the shade of your shadow

It was frozen
in the Ice Age
beaten during the Bronze Age
burned in the Dark Ages

Specified amounts of it
are used to rebuild
the points of the stars

It is the caesura
before the return
of the movement
to the dominant theme
this time in a minor key

Finally
it makes up
the long pause
at the end of the symphony
just after the climax

but before the applause

Gaudeamus Igitur: A Valediction

For this is the day of joy
   which has been fourteen hundred and sixty days in coming
For today in the breathing name of Brahms
   and the cat of Christopher Smart
   through the unbroken line of language and all the nouns
   stored in the angular gyrus
   today is a commencing
For this is the day you know too little
   against the day when you will know too much
For you will be invincible
   and vulnerable in the same breath
   which is the breath of your patients
For their breath is our breathing and our reason
For the patient will know the answer
   and you will ask him
   ask her
For the family may know the answer
For there may be no answer
   and you will know too little again
   or there *will* be an answer and you will know too much forever
For you will look smart and feel ignorant
   and the patient will not know which day it is for you
   and you will pretend to be smart out of ignorance
For you must fear ignorance more than cyanosis
For whole days will move in the direction of rain
For you will cry and there will be no one to talk to
   or no one but yourself
For you will be lonely
For you will be alone
For there is a difference
For there is no seriousness like joy
For there is no joy like seriousness
For the days will run together in gallops and the years
   go by as fast as the speed of thought
   which is faster than the speed of light
   or Superman
   or Superwoman
For you will not be Superman
For you will not be Superwoman

For you will not be Solomon
    but you will be asked the question nevertheless
For after you learn what to do, how and when to do it
    the question will be *whether*
For there will be addictions: whiskey, tobacco, love
For they will be difficult to cure
For you yourself will pass the kidney stone of pain
    and be joyful
For this is the end of examinations
For this is the beginning of testing
For Death will give the final examination
    and everyone will pass
For the sun is always right on time
    and even that may be reason for a kind of joy
For there are all kinds of
    all degrees of joy
For love is the highest joy
For which reason the best hospital is a house of joy
    even with rooms of pain and loss
    exits of misunderstanding
For there is the mortar of faith
For it helps to believe
For Mozart can heal and no one knows where he is buried
For penicillin can heal
    and the word
    and the knife
For the placebo will work and you will think you know why
For the placebo will have side effects and you will know you do not
    know why
For none of these may heal
For joy is nothing if not mysterious
For your patients will test you for spleen
    and for the four humors
For they will know the answer
For they have the disease
For disease will peer up over the hedge
    of health, with only its eyes showing
For the T waves will be peaked and you will not know why
For there will be computers
For there will be hard data and they will be hard to understand

For the trivial will trap you and the important escape you
For the Committee will be unable to resolve the question
For there will be the arts
  and some will call them
  soft data
  whereas in fact they are the hard data
  by which our lives are lived
For everyone comes to the arts too late
For you can be trained to listen only for the oboe
  out of the whole orchestra
For you may need to strain to hear the voice of the patient
  in the thin reed of his crying
For you will learn to see most acutely out of
  the corner of your eye
  to hear best with your inner ear
For there are late signs and early signs
For the patient's story will come to you
  like hunger, like thirst
For you will know the answer
  like second nature, like first
For the patient will live
  and you will try to understand
For you will be amazed
  or the patient will not live
  and you will try to understand
For you will be baffled
For you will try to explain both, either, to the family
For there will be laying on of hands
  and the letting go
For love is what death would always intend if it had the choice
For the fever will drop, the bone remold itself along
  its lines of force
  the speech return
  the mind remember itself
For there will be days of joy
For there will be elevators of elation
  and you will walk triumphantly
  in purest joy
  along the halls of the hospital
  and say *Yes* to all the dark corners

where no one is listening
For the heart will lead
For the head will explain
    but the final common pathway is the heart
    whatever kingdom may come
For what matters finally is how the human spirit is spent
For this is the day of joy
For this is the morning to rejoice
For this is the beginning
    Therefore, let us rejoice
    Gaudeamus igitur.

The moment I'm talking about
is the moment
in the ten-story department store

parking lot
at which you remember
that you don't remember

which level
where in the lot you parked
why you came in the first place

How impossible it is
to forget
the important things

How easy this is
Which brings to mind
that instant

that one year
those ten
you'd like really

both to remember
and to forget
which blessedly

is not in the scheme of things
It's the point at which you're
as they say down South

eaten up with memory
so much so that you would
scream but can't

unlike your dog
who can growl and wag
his tail at the same time

Whoever put this whole
parking lot together
knows that such ambiguity

is where
the excitement begins.

The Pigeon Sonnets

for Ron and for Keith

HOMING PIGEON I

Its house as handsome as a Henry Moore
a prisoner in the rounded sleep of egg
being embryo could be a bore:
a rudimentary heart, a wing, a leg.

But then the chipping chisel of its beak—
a burglar on the perfect inside job—
and with a novice's display of cheek
what began as instinct ends as squab.

Three weeks later mother throws a curve
forcing the youngling from the yawning nest
to fall back onto sheer ancestral nerve
and the assumption that such is for the best.

    Whether feathered or in human skin
    in the beginning the trick is to begin.

HOMING PIGEON II

Rising to risk a thousand miles away
wings whipping like a metronome
the bird circles and conjures up the way:
two days later he swoops back down—at home.

A feat of such Lindberghian *esprit*
must mystify the pigeons in the park.
It summons up no less than awe in me
pleased to find the bathroom in the dark.

Exactly how it's done remains the question:
By sleight-of-wing? By avian ESP?
I doubt that science, with intricate digestion,
will ever explicate this pedigree

    though all of us in time will have to steer
    the wordless distances from there to here.

HOMING PIGEON III

Surely, one mile up, there is the lure
of flying past the loft, of foreign intrigue,
of what might yet be his, of one detour
before clear signs of structural fatigue;

maybe taking off some Saturday
to Rio or New York or even France,
reborn into the world as emigré
all future landings left strictly to chance.

Still, though some are lost to hawks or cats
and some go down in perfect cloudless weather
most do return, ending with pirouettes
above the loft, resummoned by some tether

    like monks assembling, like most of us, reshaping
    the wondrous burden of our not escaping.

THE PIGEON IN THE PARK

Despised by breeders of the homing pigeon
this commoner is termed a "feathered rat,"
with maladies and lice, a true curmudgeon
whose genes are not for muscle, but for fat.

Nevertheless the pigeon in the square
has cooed with credit and surprising grace
in Central Park, St. Mark's, and at Trafalgar
a public service slander can't erase.

He needs no word from me in his defense
only a note of well-meant admiration
for this average waddling pestilence
who never seeks to rise above his station

> though, like the poet, he does regard as sweet
> his own erratic soarings from the street.

THE PIGEONS AT STRATFORD

As they have for centuries, the birds
still fret and strut and take their endless bows
and in this thatchèd city built of words
the keepers of the bones still keep their vows.

Though the Tourist Centers now intrude
though the buses threaten suffocation
though the usher at the play be rude
the master showman nightly draws ovation.

Yet now doth rampant Souvenir with dung
inflict upon the town a grievous stench
whilst these ancient pigeons prate among
the punkish knave, the fundamental wench

> And at the birthplace of the mortal Bard
> motorcycles curse the immortal yard.

THE DEAD PIGEON

Once in Venice, in St. Mark's, I stopped
to watch a child, a girl of two or three,
bending to study a pigeon that had dropped
dead as a duck in that pure certainty.

I think now of the other death in Venice—
of Aschenbach not rising from his chair,
of gondolas and their enduring menace,
and of the child, her wonderment and stare.

Death divides us all to shape and shadow—
pigeons, children, old men on the beach.
Those left must learn the language of the widow
to speak to those who move just out of reach

    Two have made it back, according to Word.
    Neither one was Aschenbach—or the bird.

THE (MESSENGER) PIGEON

Misdirected (I thought), a pigeon perched
at the windowsill tonight, a gray surprising
rustle in the open bay. He lurched,
bustled, and bobbed his head, as though surmising

lights meant love—and this might be the place
expecting the note (I imagine now) he carried.
Slow-witted, I tried to shoo him out of grace:
even-toed, composed, he would not be harried.

No, he tilted his head to investigate,
extending his neck to survey my room; conveying
less than a myna might of where you wait,
serene as a dove in the game (I've guessed) you're playing.

Oblique in love as a shy medieval pen,
necessary one, would you write—again?

COOING IN UNIVERSITY COLLEGE QUAD THE LOVER-PIGEON WAKES HIM UP AT 5 A.M.

The shortest way between two distances
is this quad. The bird, a baritone,
with all of Romeo's insistences,
banks pidgin-English off the ancient stone.

The lover gargles loudly, but to whom?
Amplified as through a microphone
to resonate more roundly in my room
the sum of all his sound is monotone.

I have no doubt that she will reappear:
Though it's the season to doubt everything,
that pigeons mate for life is also clear.

I move he wait her out, at least till spring:
A love is someone who can always hear
the only music you can ever sing.

It began as innocently as any birth can: moan of the mother, wail of the baby, and the father with nothing to do but wait. The child, a girl, seemed normal enough, crying enough, certainly, eating well enough to be taken home to the new nonspecific yellow nursery. Things went well, in fact, for the first several days. Then, suddenly, cough and fever, no appetite. The doctor, bless him, in the far-out stretches of the city, saw the child when it was too late for penicillin.

I have thought what it must be like to lie on your back and stare fuzzily up at the rings, triangles, bells and rattles so beloved by adults, their round faces ballooning down at you and cooing; and to know in a wordless way that you're not going to make it in this world.

The child was brought in, its trachea no larger than the tip of your little finger, the ambulance wailing for it from a long way off, all the way to the Emergency Department. The technician rushed in like a father, his pupils wide as midnight, pressing the child's chest with two fingers, just as he'd been taught, and puffing into the child's blue mouth.

*   *   *

An autopsy is the result of a human need to know. A there but for the grace of God go I kind of question and answer. This one, like all of them, was a religious ceremony, the question *why*, the answer a two-chambered heart. No sign of arteries to the lungs, only a single large vessel arising in a curve out of the abnormal heart, doing its best, which was not enough, for ten days.

How, you say, we say, could something like that have been missed? I need only refer us all to the turtle's heart, the frog's heart, that went before in the ebb of evolution: Their hearts' streamlined flow easily enough for all their slow treks, their enormous leaps.

The heart compensates for what it lacks by trying to pass for normal for as long as it can. That is never long enough. But it is still the heart's first lesson and its only language, however long it has.

Confabulation

Striding up to his bed, you
know the right questions.
Old with alcohol, yellow
as a lemon, he wrinkles

for a cigarette. He
will lie to you at a moment's
confusion, going along with you

to cover the fact that he can't
remember yesterday.

Do you remember me?

Sure I remember you.

We met in the bar at 8th
and Jackson.

Yeah, sure.

The redhead: you remember her.

Yeah, I remember.

What was her name—started with
an L . . .

Loretta? Laura?

Loretta. That's it. What a
woman. You're a lucky man to
know Loretta.

I know. I know Loretta. I'm a lucky man.

And Loretta is a lucky woman.

August: The Cricket

There's a cricket loose in the room
weaving a melancholy loom

of music, rubbing his wings together
despite this frightful August weather.

A cricket, even when it's hot,
knows what is cricket and what is not.

This persistent mournful grating
means he's interested in mating

or so I'm told—that's why he sings,
scraping a chord along his wings.

Sound seems to come from everywhere
(though when you look he isn't there).

He makes a rather nice career
trying to lure a female near.

His constant chirping almost begs
her to listen with her legs.

Now, thinking she's not in the mood,
he decides to go for food—

a piece of wool, a recent book
on poetry or how to cook.

Despite his inauspicious start
a book or two might help his art

and one of them provide the word:
most music made is never heard.

Argument and After

silence
first

then words
teeth

wrath tongue
and fire beneath

tears a laugh
touch calm

love opens
its fist

is again
a palm

In the first grade
for this unit
we are studying
The Age of the Dinosaurs
We are also making
an exhibit to be shown
at PTA

Everyone except Johnny
wanted to make
a Stegosaurus
or a Tyrannosaurus rex
out of clay

Johnny preferred to make
a Brontosaurus
which explains

why the demography
of our dinosaur population
may seem somewhat
out of kilter

Nevertheless
the whole class
has been involved
in this demonstration
and we are almost ready
to represent
several hundred millennia

using a backdrop of green
posterboard, the dinosaur
models, of course

and at least a hundred
small clay pellets
meant to be eggs
and not whatever
petrified else
you may have been thinking
they were

By working together
we have learned much
in the preparation
of this interesting exhibit

which may yet win
First Prize
and make our inscrutable parents
proud at last

We thought of having
special music
to go with our
display
but we couldn't agree
as a class

on just what kind of music
dinosaurs
might have preferred

while on their way
to what everyone knows
came next:

a big fat zero

To tell you the truth
the whole thing
leaves me
a little sad

the way
every day
always
somewhere
sometime
someone

is having to start all over

1. EARLY

The earliest leaves are now
starting to fall. Those
that did contrive somehow

in autumn's swift revision
to cling a moment more
have turned in pure precision

burned yellow, brown,
red, ochre, gold
in every part of town

as though replying to
a question I never heard.
If color is a clue

I take all this to mean
whatever the answer was
it couldn't be said in green.

2. LATE

"Hope" is the thing with
feathers
—Emily Dickinson

Out in the weather
the waterproof birds
hoping together
exempted from words

this is my time
the fall of the leaf
that imperfect crime
finale of grief

summer's illusion
a figure of speech
August's intrusion
cast off on the beach

December ahead
white as the distance
frost overspread
at winter's insistence

the chances of spring
little more than a guess
whatever the question
the answer is *yes.*

How long have I known this man, I thought, my head bowed, the crying over, done with, here in the hospital room; how long have I known this patient, this boy; this 22-year-old stretched out and quietly not breathing in the dark room. Raining outside. Seventeen years.

*   *   *   *   *

I first met David when he was five. I was then a Cardiology Fellow, learning how the heart works, how it goes wrong. I became his doctor some 10 years ago and over that time I came to think of him as something of a heroic figure. He'd been through three major orthopedic operations, two of them on his spine. And four years ago, the open-heart surgery that had allowed him to go back to school, to study microchips, computers, and other paraphernalia I know less and less about. He got on well after the surgery: quaffed a few on Saturday nights, went camping, went to the mountains. The trip he recalled with the greatest pleasure was one to the Gulf coast: he never forgot those five days with a college buddy, spent fishing, crabbing, cooking and eating. He liked the slower pace of that small town and told me later it was the kind of place he'd want to settle down in: the people there really knew how to live. I knew his heart wasn't perfect, never would be perfect. But there is, within the nation of Cardiology, the state of Perfect Enough: whatever works.

*   *   *   *   *

A month ago, almost matter-of-factly, after my office examination, he said that he was just a bit more short of breath. Not much, just a bit. A bit tired after climbing a flight of stairs. Still sleeping flat. Comfortable at rest. Maybe he was just putting on too much weight. Over the next few weeks, though, he got worse. He saw his family doctor with symptoms that sounded like flu, bronchitis. He seemed at first to respond to antibiotics. Cough got better. But then heart failure bore in on him. Air hunger. Having to sit up to catch his breath. And so he called me, or his mother called, and I admitted him to the hospital.

*   *   *   *   *

In this same hospital, four years before, he lay after his open-heart surgery, with pain at every breath because of the knife, his new heart

42

valve working well. Post-op and sick. Breathing hard. But finally, as his mother and I watched, he began to come round. A little better every day. Tubes all out. Fever coming down without antibiotics. Stronger. Wanted a hamburger; a good sign, maybe the best sign. He strolled with me in the hall, nodding to the nurses, smiling gamely, talking about Dungeons and Dragons. He went back to school and did well: made the Dean's List one quarter and was very proud.

* * * * *

But now heart failure had descended on him like the plague. He had to work hard to breathe. In the Emergency Department, one of the Residents met me and helped me get an IV line in. The Resident was a physician I'd taken care of, several years ago, when he himself was sick and had to be hospitalized. I told David that the Resident never could get used to needles; he'd rebelled against needles, against my ordering too many blood tests. That seemed to reassure David, who only grimaced as the needle slipped into his own vein.

* * * * *

Over the next few days he improved. The treatment seemed to be working. He lost several pounds of fluid, began breathing easier. Sleeping flat. But almost as suddenly as it left, his difficulty came back. Tore into him with force. With recruitments. And he had to sit up again in order to breathe. Struggling for air. We got a scan of his heart and the confirmatory bad news. His heart was much bigger than it should be, barely pumping on the scan, pumping perhaps a third of what it should. Just enough to keep him alive.

* * * * *

I told his mother. Indirectly, I told David. Yes, the scan did show serious disease. Yes, I thought there were some things we could do to help him. No, we weren't licked yet. But I was afraid we were.

* * * * *

Morphine: a godsend. It works wonders. It does good things for the heart and the head. Though only temporarily, it brings respite from the heart failure. Slows the work of breathing, unloads the heart. It takes away the sensation of shortness of breath caused by fluid building up in the lungs, eases for a couple of hours or more the feeling of suffocation. Morphine works quickly and its actions are blessèd: if you are still short of breath, you no longer care. You sleep. You dream.

*   *   *   *   *

On morning rounds today, David told me he'd seen some strange things outside his room in the middle of the night. He said he knew they weren't there. I asked him what kinds of things he saw. Dogs, he said; dogs and cats and a clown. I knew they weren't there, he said, because this is a hospital. Was it frightening? I asked. No, not frightening; it was kind of interesting. He'd been in the bustling beeping ICU too many days. But at least he'd recognized these hallucinations for what they were—or were not. We talked for a long time. He said he thought the new medicine was helping a bit. And the morphine really helps me, he said. Yes.

*   *   *   *   *

On my way out of the ICU, his mother called me into the waiting room. I told her about the dogs and cats and the clown. I told her I was worried. She was worn out from several straight nights spent between the waiting room and the ICU, smoothing back his sweaty hair, pouring soft drinks for him. Just being there. She and David had had a little tiff this morning, she said. She'd told him that she had to go home for a while. Had to. Had to get a bath. Stretch out in a bed for a few hours so that she could come back and continue to be with him. I agreed with her. She was red-eyed, exhausted. He didn't want her to leave him, of course. They'd argued briefly about that. She said to me, do you think he knows he's dying? Yes. Yes, I said. He knows; without being told. I wrote two Latin words on a 3 × 5 card for her: *angor animi*—Suetonius' phrase. It means the fear of impending doom, anguish of the spirit. Patients know. Yes, I said, he knows. But she did need to go home. She was no good here: to him or to herself. I sent her off.

*   *   *   *   *

At three o'clock, the office phone rang. It was the ICU nurse. David was worse; his blood pressure had fallen. Did I have any suggestions. I'll come, I said, slipping out the office door and walking briskly through the rain the one block to the hospital. Off the elevator and into the ICU. Oh, doctor; good, he said, as I came in. What's the matter, David? He was taking off the oxygen mask. Keep that on,

David, you need it. He lay back on the bed, exhausted, sweating, his chest racked with the effort of breathing, the incredible energy of staying alive. As he lay down, his eyes rolled back just a bit too far in his head. I knew I had to call his mother. I went to the phone and dialed her quickly. She was on her way. I strode back into his room just as one of the nurses was coming out to get me, her face anxious. David had slumped further down and was taking a last quiet attempt at a breath. There was some initial flurry of activity around the bed, some confusion; the bag-valve-mask was put over his face and he was given some oxygen. But he was gone. No question. No more breaths on his own. I put my stethoscope on his chest. No movement of the chest. His EKG monitor was still going, but no breaths. I put the stethoscope back in my pocket, crossed my forearms on the bed rail, and the tears began welling up. I turned toward the window; raining outside. The staff had known what to expect; we'd talked at length: no heroics. No attempts at resuscitation. Let him go. Gracefully. Quietly. Which he had done. The tears came, the muffled noises in the throat, the sobs and gulpings, for several minutes. When I opened my eyes again, the staff had left the room, turning out the lights as they left. David lay peacefully. Like the *Pietà*, I thought, but waiting for his mother. I closed his eyes. We both waited.

*   *   *   *   *

One of the nurses who'd known David well, who'd cared for him for days and days, came into the room. We talked for a few minutes about his death, what needed to be done: details. Then, at the same time, we were both aware of an incongruity: the cardiac monitor, the EKG, was still showing some electrical activity. The cardiac impulses were still marching along across the screen in their electrical sweep. Should I turn off the monitor, she asked? Yes, I said, automatically. Yes. *No. No, wait. Turn it back on.* The EKG started its sweep across again. *Leave it on. His mother's on her way.* A minute later she came into the room. She already knew. *Angor animi.* She knew. Expected. Oh, David, my precious David, she said, gathering him to her, cradling him. Those are his last few beats, Judy, I said, pointing to the monitor. Just at that moment, as she looked, his heart stopped completely. He waited for you. She nodded, as though she'd expected that also. And perhaps she had. But I hadn't.

The Circuit

You despise checking out
of hotel rooms
especially the going back

for one more look around.
There's always the feeling
you've left something behind.

That's because you have.

December

At the bottom of the hill
on which stands
one of the grandest houses

in town
past which I drive daily
on my way to tend

the sickest poor
in town
a woman in a blue

silk dressing gown
just before Christmas
is vigorously poking

a long stick
down into two huge rolling
garbage cans

which she has just brought out
to the curb
from the house

poking the stick down
hard so that the tops
will fit the cans

so that some degree
of equanimity
may attend the day.

By such incongruities
is the free world
saved.

The Bass

Because I was 37 and he was 10
I was presumed and of course
to know everything important

plus
how to take the fish off the hook.
I'd been told largemouth

and striped bass
both   either
waited for us below

the still crystal of the lake
I had no expectation though
of actually catching a fish

when somehow we did
After we hauled it heavily
in over the gunwales

like a glittering glory
no way was I about to touch
that wide mouth, those razor fins

gills, those sparkling cold-blooded
scales
until all spasm stopped

To this day my son
may think the way
to take a fish off the hook

is to place it, hook still intact
in the bottom of the boat
place a paddle over the fish

and keep your foot gently but steadfastly
on the paddle on the fish
After the flailing and flopping

I managed with something like
experience to get the hook out
Then as morning broke over us

we made our slow electric way
back to the boathouse
That fish won for us

a trophy
which I keep here on my desk
to remind me of that morning and of .

how unexpected the end may be
how hungry
how shining